HOUSES AND HOMES

PENNY MARSHALL

Macdonald

941

Jacket pictures

Front(main): A Welsh shepherd and family at home, 1950
Front(small): Park Hill Estate, Sheffield, 1970s
Back(top): Family group with servants, Ketteringham, Norfolk, 1865
Back(bottom): Going out for a walk, New Malden, Surrey, 1950

A MACDONALD BOOK

First published in 1985 by
Macdonald & Co. (Publishers) Ltd
London and Sydney

Reprinted 1986

© Macdonald & Co. (Publishers) Ltd 1985

ISBN 0 356 10145 2

Macdonald & Co. (Publishers) Ltd
Maxwell House
74 Worship Street
London EC2A 2EN

A BPCC PLC company

Printed by Purnell Book Production Ltd
Paulton, Bristol.

BRITISH LIBRARY CATALOGUING IN PUBLICATION DATA

Marshall, Penny
 Houses and homes.–(The camera as witness)
 1. Housing–Great Britain–History
 –Juvenile literature
 I. Title   II. Series
 363.5′0941   HD7333.A3

ISBN 0-356-10145-2

CREDITS

Aerofilms Ltd: 30(top)
Aldus Archive: 5
Barnaby's Picture Library: 18, 36,
 42(bottom)
BBC Hulton Picture Library: title page,
 8(top and bottom), 26, 27, 29, 35
Bromley Central Library: 32, 33(top,
 centre and bottom)
Edinburgh City Libraries: 21
Courtesy of Mr A. Frost: 7 (top and
 bottom)
GLC: 25
Leicestershire Museums: 20(top)
Manchester Polytechnic: 37(top), © Mrs
 Ingham
Manchester Public Libraries: 16(top and
 bottom), 22, 44(top)
Mansell Collection: back cover (top), 9,
 11
Mitchell Library, Glasgow: 20(bottom)
Newcastle City Libraries: 12(bottom),
 13, 23, 28
Graham Ovenden: 17
Topham: front cover(main and inset),
 back cover(bottom), 4(Victoria &
 Albert Museum), 14(top and bottom),
 19(bottom), 24, 30(bottom), 31, 34,
 37(bottom), 38, 39(top and bottom),
 40, 41(top and bottom), 42(top), 43
Tower Hamlets Central Library: 12(top)
Vestry House Museum: 10, 44(bottom)
Victoria & Albert Museum: 6
Welholme Galleries: 19(top)
West Sussex County Record Office:
 15(top and bottom)

Picture research by Diana Morris

Camdean School

Contents

Introduction

In the 1850s, when this book starts, railways were still quite new, cars had not been invented, flying was a fantasy and reaching the moon beyond the wildest dreams. Today's comfortable homes and labour-saving appliances were also beyond most people's imagination.

As you will see from the photographs in this book, the contrast then between the way the rich and the poor lived was far greater than anything we know today. This was largely because there were more very rich people and more very poor people than there are now.

The houses of the rich were large, crammed with furniture, and inconvenient – though that was more of a problem for the servants who had to work in the houses than for the families whose homes they were. The houses of the poor were tiny, cramped and inconvenient, largely because they lacked the most basic amenities. It was quite usual for a dozen or so houses to share one tap, and one 'privy' or outside lavatory.

Many visitors to England in the nineteenth century commented on the contrast, pointing out the appalling poverty that could be found only a few minutes' walk from a city's fashionable shopping areas.

The increasing pressures for social reform towards the end of the nineteenth century forced governments to act to improve conditions. But until 1919, when housing became the responsibility of local authorities, with financial assistance from the government, improvements were haphazard.

As home amenities, such as water, gas and electricity, became more complicated, the need for better planned houses was obvious. This was helped by the decline in the number of servants. Job opportunities for women had increased so much by the 1920s that few now wanted to be servants.

Home furnishings reflect this change, too. When there were plenty of servants to dust and sweep and polish, fussy, crowded rooms were popular. But as more and more housewives had to do more and more of that work themselves, and now frequently go out to work as well, furnishings have become much more simple. Central heating has replaced messy coal fires, stainless steel has superseded silver, and wipe-clean surfaces have almost done away with the scrubbing brush.

Houses today are certainly much easier to look after; they are also a lot more comfortable to live in, with luxuries such as indoor bathrooms, hot water and electric lighting that would have been undreamed of by most of the people in this book.

HOW TO USE THIS BOOK

The photos in this book give a good idea of the changes in the houses and homes that people have lived in over the last century and a quarter, and also of how little some things have changed.

As you read through the book, look out for the things that are different from today, and also for the things that are the same. You can tell, too, from people's expressions what they are thinking, and that certainly hasn't changed!

Learn to look closely at the photographs and to draw conclusions from what you see. Although they were never intended as such, all the photographs in this book are important documents in our social history.

The date at the top of each page tells you when the photograph was taken.

A NOTE ABOUT PHOTOGRAPHY

In the 1850s, when this book starts, photography was very much a new and unusual hobby, a pastime for a few scientifically-minded amateurs with servants to carry the heavy, cumbersome equipment. Taking photographs was a laborious process. The sitter had to stay still for several minutes while the image was exposed on the photographic plate. Any movement, however slight, would come out as a blur.

Early photographs were processed onto metal and glass as well as paper. Improvements came first through the experiments of individuals, usually working alone to solve problems. Early great pioneers included William Henry Fox Talbot, Frederick Scott Archer and the Frenchman, Louis Daguerre. Their discoveries made photography what it is today.

With today's cameras it is possible for anyone to take a photo – just point the camera and snap! But that hasn't reduced photography's important role as a recorder of history – the history of individuals as well as great events. Every photograph, however ordinary, can be considered an historical document. As you will discover in this book, there is a lot you can learn from a photograph!

The photograph below was taken in 1907. Cameras were already much simpler than in the very early days of photography, but were still slow and difficult to use.

Eynsford in Kent (left), photographed in 1859 by the famous Victorian photographer, Francis Bedford, is typical of many English villages. The houses are grouped by a small river. The woman getting water by the bridge tells us that this is an important source of water for the village. The cart tracks in the mud indicate that the river is shallow and the bridge too narrow for the horse-drawn carts that were the chief form of transport. Notice the small windows and large chimney stacks on the houses, as well as all the timber they used. And there are, of course, no television aerials, telephone wires or cars.

FORE STREET, LAMBETH

Fore Street in Lambeth, south London, seen here in 1860, is more of an alley than a street. There are no drains. Instead, the roughly cobbled surface of the street slopes slightly down from the buildings so that when it rains the water will run down the middle of the alley, carrying with it all sorts of smelly refuse.

Streets like this were common in all Britain's major cities at this time. As industries developed and more people came from country areas to live in the towns, housing became more and more of a problem.

Houses were put up very quickly, and as many crammed into a small area as possible to try and save money.

The houses open directly on to the street. There were no front gardens and no back gardens. Often there was not even a tiny backyard, because the houses in one street backed directly onto the backs of the houses in the next street.

As a result the rooms in houses like these were very dark, as well as being small. And the two gas street lights would not have brightened the

street much at night.

Although the street seems deserted, these poor houses were homes to more people than we would now believe possible. Three of the inhabitants are in the photo - can you spot them? Hanging just below the top window on the right is a cage with a pet bird. Perhaps it belongs to the person with the blurred face looking out of the window.

KELVEDON

Until the Industrial Revolution, at the end of the eighteenth century, most people in Britain lived in country areas. The high street at Kelvedon in Essex, photographed here in 1862, is typical of old country towns and villages. But with the growth of great industrial cities in the nineteenth century, 'home' for most people became a noisy, dirty city. Increasingly, children were growing up in streets like Fore Street (opposite) rather than high streets like Kelvedon's.

Both the photographs on this page were taken on the same day and looking in the same direction. Can you spot the gas lamp-post and the pub sign for 'Richmond's Superior Home-brew'd Ale' in each picture? You can tell from this where the photographs overlap.

Notice the unsurfaced road. Clearly there has been a spell of dry weather. Everything was still horse-drawn and would continue to be for nearly half a century, and the narrow wheels of the carts have left trails in the dust. In wet weather the wheels will leave deep ruts in the mud.

Look at the little house beside the pub in the top picture. One of its window shutters flaps upward over the window, not across as the others do. The side of this house is faced with clapboard – wooden planks. Clapboard is still quite common in Essex. Elsewhere in East Anglia, many of the houses were built of flint stones, and the roofs thatched with reeds, not tiled as here.

Variations like these reflect what building materials were available locally – there were no heavy lorries to transport materials over long distances. Watch out for these variations, both in the photos in this book and when you are out in the country or the old parts of today's towns and cities.

AT THE PIANO

This scene is carefully posed so that no-one moves and spoils the finished picture.

The girl at the piano cannot play it while the photo is being taken. Cameras at this time were still very 'slow', and it took a few minutes for the image of the scene being photographed to register on the glass photographic plate (film as we know it had not yet been invented). If anyone moved during that time they showed just as a blur in the final picture.

The way the girls are dressed, with their ringlets, bows, flowers, lace and frills, echoes the fussy effect of the room. Look at the patterned wallpaper, and the curtains behind the piano with a quite different pattern.

Ornaments covered by glass domes, like the one on the piano, were very popular in Victorian homes. You can sometimes see them today in antique shops.

Until the invention of radio, hi-fi and television, playing the piano and singing were favourite ways to spend a family evening.

A FAMILY TEA

This Victorian family are enjoying tea and fruit cake. The plates look quite delicate, and the large cups, too, are made of china – colourful earthenware mugs were many years away.

The wallpaper seems very dark, and the reproductions of well-known paintings hanging on the walls are in equally heavy frames – bright prints and stainless steel frames, or even no frames, are a very modern idea.

The chair on the left was a popular style in Victorian times, and they are still quite common. But oil lamps like the one in the centre of the table were much more fragile and so fewer have survived.

VICTORIAN INTERIOR

What a clutter, we would probably think today. But to the Victorians, the barer rooms we are used to would seem very empty.

There's so much detail in this photograph that it's worth looking at it very closely. See how the decoration at the top of the walls echoes the style of the 'Persian' carpet on the floor. The room is lit by oil lamps, though the heavy cover over the central one must have blocked out most of the light. The small ones each side of the fireplace have different patterns on their glass globes – no matching pairs here.

The heavy curtains at the fireplace help to reduce the draught from the chimney when the coal fire is not alight. Coal fires make a lot of ash, and the grate has to be cleaned out every day before the fire is lit. Think how dusty all these ornaments must get from the fine ash.

Servants are there to keep them clean, of course – in many middle-class homes there were often as many servants as members of the family. Even so it was no joke keeping rooms like these spotless, especially when you remember there were no labour-saving devices, just dustpan and brush, mop and broom.

PLAYING CROQUET

This game of croquet is taking place in a suburb in the north-east of London, but houses and gardens like this were typical of prosperous middle-class areas throughout Queen Victoria's reign (1837-1901). Notice how the left-hand part of the house is set across the end of the right-hand part. The roof is not as steeply pitched, and is covered with slates rather than tiles. It is probably an addition.

Small covered verandahs with steps down to the garden were a feature of many houses at this period. 'French windows' – really doors with panes of glass in them instead of wooden panels – lead from the drawing-room on to the verandah.

Notice how the open French windows have net curtains drawn across them. There are blinds, too, across some of the other windows. Both blinds and curtains were there to keep sunlight out of the rooms. The dyes used for fabrics such as chair coverings were not fast as they are today, and materials faded quickly in strong sunlight. The little windows in the roof which are open and have no blinds probably belong to the servants, and any curtains and bedspreads there are likely to be old and faded already.

A BEDROOM

This bedroom (right) shows that the Victorians' love of clutter was not confined to sitting-rooms (page 9).

Look at all the things in the photograph: the splendid brass bedstead, the big pillow, the marble-topped washstand in the corner with its water jugs and bowls, the ceramic slop bucket with the cane handle on the floor beside it, the pictures, the armchairs and couch, and the carpets – there are at least three, apart from the hearthrug. Notice, too, that the ceiling has a patterned paper on it in a very different style to the wallpaper.

At the top of the nearest window you can just see a rolled up blind, for use at night and on sunny days.

Have you noticed that, reflected in the mirror over the fireplace, you can see the end of the room where the photographer is standing?

BETHNAL GREEN

Bethnal Green is a poor part of east London today, just as it was when this photograph of Lamb Gardens (above) was taken in 1870.

The chimney pots on these tiny single-storey cottages are cracked and broken. There is little guttering and no drainpipes, so that when it rains the water will just run off the roof and make puddles on the ground. The narrow brick extension on the right, with its broken tiles on the roof, is the outside lavatory or 'privy'. It is shared by several of the cottages.

Social reformers were beginning to realize that such housing was harmful. Throughout Britain, rows of cottages like this were gradually being replaced by blocks of flats (page 16).

But although the people of Lamb Gardens are clearly very poor, they are luckier than some. They have gardens and so can grow fruit and vegetables. One of the gardens here is very productive. They also 'grew' their own meat – the slatted wooden structures are rabbit hutches. And the rabbit skins would fetch a few much-needed pence. Life was far too tough for the people of Lamb Gardens to think of rabbits as pets.

NEWCASTLE SLUMS

The people of Bethnal Green were poor, but in some ways they were luckier than poor people living in the centres of industrial cities. There was nowhere for these people in the slums of Newcastle (left and right) to grow vegetables or rear rabbits. The picture on the left, taken in 1884, shows a narrow alley in the city's slum area. The photograph on the right, taken two years later, shows the back of a similar slum.

At least the houses on the left have been whitewashed quite recently, and the buildings are of stone and brick. At the back (right) it is quite a different story. Most of the walls have wooden frames filled with lath and plaster (slats of wood padded with plaster), but look how the plaster is crumbling away. The yard is uneven with rubble and rubbish, and none of the doors or windows fit properly, so there is no chance of keeping out draughts.

Barefooted children were a very common sight in slums like these. Even the boots the adults are wearing are probably second- or third-hand.

The four photographs shown here were all taken in the 1890s, but what a contrast they make.

A KITCHEN

(Right) It is 25 minutes to five and preparations for the evening meal are under way in the kitchen of Burton House near Petworth in Sussex. On the table is a joint of beef – a favourite Victorian dish – and the cook on the left is rolling out pastry.

Look at the dresser with its huge array of pots and pans. From the way they shine they are probably made of copper. The lids, which are hanging from the dresser shelves, are flat – very like the lids of pans still used in restaurant kitchens.

Clamped to the edge of the table is a large mincer – electric food processors are a modern invention. The kitchen floor looks a bit scuffed and uneven because it is covered with sand. This absorbed any spilt liquid and was easy to sweep up. Sometimes sawdust was used instead.

WASHERWOMEN

(Left) In the days before washing machines and launderettes everyone who could afford it paid someone else to do their washing. Big houses had their own laundries (opposite) while middle-class homes often had someone who came in just to do the washing. In poorer areas you usually took the laundry to a washerwoman such as the ones photographed here in Whitby, Yorkshire.

Doing the laundry was hard work. The only real labour-saving device was the mangle. The woman on the right is wringing the washing before it goes through the mangle to get the rest of the water out. Imagine washing sheets (there were no easy-care fabrics) without today's machines to help. It is not surprising that these women have large, powerful arms and big hands.

GRINDING CORN

The woman above is grinding corn she and her husband have grown in their little fields on the Isle of Skye, off the west coast of Scotland. The crop is probably oats – modern types of wheat that can withstand damp and short growing seasons had not yet been developed.

The stick she is using to turn the grindstone is supported by a bar and rope set in the wall, and you can see that stick is black from years of use.

In the background is their little stone-walled house. The thatch is held down by ropes weighted with stones to prevent the winter storms from ripping it off the roof. But why do you think there is a pair of boots on the roof?

THE LAUNDRY

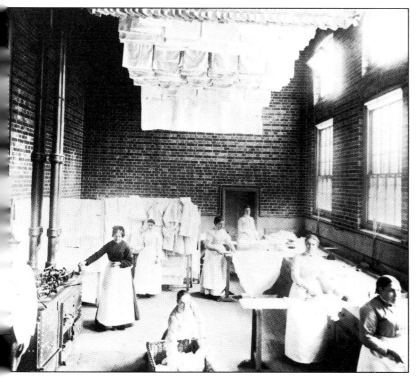

(Left) This is the laundry room at Petworth House in Sussex. You can tell what a large household it serves by the number of staff – seven women, and a man to stoke the boilers for the hot water.

The boilers are on the left and on them flat irons are warming. There were no thermostatically controlled irons then. Instead you heated the iron on the boiler or kitchen range, or beside the fire, holding it near your cheek to check whether it was hot enough to use. When it was ready another iron was put on to heat so it could be used when the first iron had cooled. One of the girls on the right is ironing a child's dress.

Rows of clean laundry hang from the ceiling. Although the room must be very hot, all the laundresses are wearing high-necked dresses, and only one has even rolled up her long sleeves.

TENEMENTS

Throughout the 1880s and 1890s tenement blocks like these ones here in Manchester were slowly replacing the slums (pages 12 and 13). The top picture shows the view from the inside courtyard, while the outside is shown on the left. Although they are not the same building, you can see from the arched doorway and the chimney stacks how very similar they are in construction.

'Corporation dwellings' like these became a feature of all industrial towns. They look very forbidding, more like barracks than homes. This partly reflected the Victorians' view that life should not be made easy for poor people be-

A GARDEN PARTY

cause it would encourage them to be lazy and not try to find work.

The balconies at least provided a covered place to hang the washing. And in the centre of the block there is an open space for children to play in, which also means that the flats are quite light. Someone here has even thought of planting ornamental trees in tubs. We are so used to open play areas and streets planted with trees that it is hard to realize what an unusual and imaginative step this was in 1894.

Homes with gardens large enough for a marquee and with plenty of room to spare were beyond the wildest dreams of the people who lived in the tenements opposite. In just the same way, these people in their smart clothes enjoying this splendid garden party could not have imagined life in small dark rooms without servants to do all the hard work.

The photograph is undated and the party is probably to celebrate some family event – an engagement, a christening or a special anniversary. On the other hand, the strings of flags suggest that it may have been taken at a party to celebrate the coronation of King Edward

VII in August 1902.

The day is fine and it is parasols, not umbrellas, that are being used. But in view of the British climate it was a wise precaution to have the buffet table set out in the small marquee. It is a pity, though, that it is impossible to see the food. Following the example of their king, wealthy Edwardians enjoyed good food and a standard of living that we have never equalled since.

17

TEA OUTSIDE

These relaxed and leisured ladies are enjoying a tea that they have not prepared, outside a large, comfortable house that they do not have to keep clean.

They could sit at ease because their homes were being run by servants. Certainly, they supervised the servants, but it was not they who polished the fine teapot, made the cakes for tea, kept the lace curtains clean, or washed, starched and ironed their blouses with their innumerable lacy frills.

At the beginning of the Edwardian period, when this photograph was taken, there were about 2½ million female domestic servants in Britain. And it was quite usual for a middle-class family of three adults (husband and wife, and an unmarried daughter) to have a staff of three servants: a cook, a housemaid and a maid of all work. Really rich families, like those living at Petworth and Burton House (page 15), had many more, but that was because the houses themselves were so huge that many people were needed just to keep them clean and in good repair.

The little bamboo table and three-legged table are forerunners of today's outdoor furniture; but notice how deck chairs have hardly changed.

Cameras and film have improved since the earliest photographs in this book. Even though the little dog is clearly very good at begging, it would probably have looked blurred in early photographs because it would be very difficult for it to hold that position without moving and so spoiling the picture.

LAYING THE TABLE

These two maids (above) are preparing their employer's dining-room for a special occasion. Look at the table decorations, the starched tablecloth and the tall folded napkins. There also seems to be a bottle for each place setting!

The odd chairs at the end of the table suggest that the party will be larger than usual and that chairs have been brought in from the kitchen or nursery.

Although this room does not have the dark wallpaper of some of the earlier rooms shown in this book, dark colours are obviously still fashionable. The sideboard, with its ornaments, fruit dish and soda siphon, is in dark wood; and look at the dark carved clock-case.

Can you see the corner-cupboard with its display of the family's 'best' china?

GIRLS SINGING

Without radio or television, Victorian and Edwardian families made their own entertainment, and singing at the piano was one of the most popular. This scene (left), photographed in 1902, could be in any middle-class home in the country. Even quite poor homes had a piano, though in general it was only the middle and upper classes who had the time to develop any skill at singing or playing.

HANGING OUT THE WASHING

(Above) Washday in a Leicestershire village photographed at the beginning of this century. It looks very attractive – thatched roofs, climbing plants and lovely clean white aprons. But is it really? There are great holes in the woman's sacking apron, some of the spars holding the thatch are loose and broken, the plaster on the outbuilding looks cracked, and the thick plants climbing up the house walls probably made it very damp.

There were slum homes in country areas just as there were in the cities. In fact water supplies and sanitation in the country were often worse, because it was expensive to put in pipes and sewers to isolated villages. And all too often the exteriors, which were certainly much more attractive than those on pages 12 and 13, lulled the increasing number of social reformers into thinking that the only housing problems were in cities.

GRANNY WILSON

Sadly, the original of this photograph is damaged, so much of the detail is lost. Nevertheless it is a lovely photograph of old Granny Wilson sitting beside her hearth in the Springburn district of Glasgow. You can just see the big kettle on the fire and the oven door to the left. In those days, putting a pot on the fire was the only way to heat it. The old lady's gnarled hands tell of a lifetime of hard work, with few opportunities to sit quietly by the fire in cap and shawl.

FISHERMEN'S COTTAGES

These fishermen's children were photographed outside their homes in New Lane, Newhaven, near Edinburgh. The three girls in the middle of the street are obviously posing for the photographer, even though some of the other children are ignoring him.

The brick and stone cottages are tiny, and the small windows suggest the rooms are very dark. Built out from the front of each cottage are the lavatories, or 'closets' as they were often called. There is one at the top of the steps for the families living in the top half of the cottages and one on the ground floor for the people living there.

In wet weather rubbish and refuse probably ran down the central channel in the cobbled street.

In the foreground are some of the wooden 'buckets' and willow baskets in which the fishermen carried their catch to market.

1900s

THE NURSEMAID

(Opposite) Outside Number 89 Jesmond Road, Newcastle, stands the nursemaid with her two charges – the children of one of the city's prosperous business or professional men. Substantial three-storey houses like this were typical of well-to-do areas of towns and cities in late Victorian and Edwardian times, and this house probably has a drawing room much like the one on the left.

Notice the net curtains and wooden Venetian blinds at the windows of both houses. Although it is winter, with short days, sunlight is still something to protect against (see page 10).

The dark lines all over the front of Number 89 are the remains of last year's Virginia creeper. In the summer its glossy green leaves will hide the house's rather dingy brickwork, discoloured by smoke from the city's many factories – laws controlling air pollution are very new.

The attics in Number 87 are lit only by skylights (you can see two in the roof), but a proper dormer window has been put in at Number 89. Perhaps this is the room where the nursemaid sleeps.

You can still see houses like this in many parts of the country, but they are now usually divided into flats. The fine railings will probably no longer exist, taken during the Second World War (1939-45) to provide iron for essential war equipment.

A FIREPLACE

What a dark and gloomy room this is! Look at the dark marble mantelpiece, dark tiles around the fire, dark patterned wallpaper, with another pattern above the picture rail and yet another, smaller one on the ceiling.

Even the ornaments are heavy and dark. The mirror has a dark wooden frame, the clock is dark and so are most of the statues and vases.

The frame of the big picture on the right is probably golden, but its fussy design echoes the general feeling of clutter throughout the room.

The gas lighting (you can see one of the globes of the central light in the top righthand corner) did little to brighten the room. And the coal fire would not have helped much either, as the grate is very small.

WATERING PLANTS

This woman's home is not as grand as the one on the previous page. She lives in a prosperous working-class area, where the houses are smaller and more crowded together. The view from her back window probably looks like the photo opposite.

The armchair behind her is made of cane – there is a similar one on page 18, but there it is being used as outdoor furniture. This woman probably does not even have a garden.

The wallpaper is still boldly patterned, but it does not seem quite as dark as earlier ones. The curtains have a different pattern and so does the tablecloth, but perhaps she embroidered that herself.

The plants she is watering so carefully are ferns. These were very popular houseplants with the Victorians and Edwardians. Houses were much colder then than they are now. Ferns, which do not like the heat, thrived in the cool dark rooms. Notice, too, that they are in terracotta flowerpots – there was no plastic then. And why is there that quaint little trellis round the edge of the table? Perhaps it is to stop the children from knocking her plants over? Or the cat?

The large book on the right is probably a Bible. Most homes still had a large, leather-bound family Bible, although the practice of family prayers each evening was no longer as common as it had been.

ROOFTOPS

This photograph was taken in Marylebone, London, but it could be in almost any of the country's industrial cities in the early years of this century.

It's a very dreary outlook. You can see how some people have tried to brighten their backyards by whitewashing the brick walls, but the effect does not last long because of the air pollution. All the houses have coal fires – you can see smoke coming from two of the chimney pots. Fires like this meant smoke and smuts, as did factory chimneys and steam trains, so it is not surprising that everything looks dingy – including the washing.

Notice the large building beyond the row of houses on the left. This is one of the many types of 'improved homes for workers' built by nineteenth-century social reformers to replace the worst city slums. Although in many ways they were as grim as they look, they did have a few advantages. The drainpipes at the end of the building, for example, show that the block had indoor lavatories.

This was certainly an improvement, as most of the houses in this photograph only had outside ones. Among the clutter of shed roofs in each backyard is the one for the outside lavatory, or 'privy' as it was often called.

25

A CHRISTMAS TEA

There's no doubt what time of year this is – the decorations and great bunch of holly are all the clues you need to know that it's Christmas, in a country farmhouse in the early years of this century.

Three generations of a farming family are gathered here for Christmas tea. An unmarried labourer who works on the farm and lives with the farmer and his wife sits in a chair in the corner.

Everyone except the old farmer and the labourer are in their best clothes. The young men are wearing shirts and ties, and the women have brought out their treasured lace collars to put on their dresses for the occasion. When the day is over they will remove the lace, which is just tacked in place, and carefully put it away until the next special occasion.

Everyone is sitting quietly while the man at the end of the table says 'grace' and the photographer takes his picture. Then it will be time to enjoy the home-made cakes and jam. The milk in the cut-glass jug near the oil lamp is probably from the farm's own cows.

The room has a fairly low ceiling – the dresser on the far wall only just fits in under the beams. And you can also see that the ceiling is really the floorboards of the room above. That is something you generally only see in old houses in the country.

TEA-TIME

This is an ordinary, everyday family tea photographed in 1910. The father of the family is probably a clerk in a city office, with an annual income of around £250. This was quite a reasonable income and you could live quite comfortably on it, as long as the family was not too large. But already this couple have six children, and from the smock the wife is wearing it would seem she is pregnant with the seventh, so it will probably be increasingly difficult for them to make ends meet if he is not promoted.

Behind the wife you can see the kettle heating on the boiler, and beside it is the big, shiny family teapot.

You can still find teapots like this today. To the right behind her is the oven door. Along the mantelpiece there is a fine array of ornaments – all of which will catch the dirt every day when she cleans out the grate, and so need regular dusting.

The wallpaper is quite different from any in the photographs so far. The twisting lines in the border just above the man's head show the influence of the new Art Nouveau designs that were becoming popular, although the rest of the furniture is very traditional – and quite cheap.

Husband and wife each have a rocking chair beside the hearth – you can just see the tip of one of the rockers on the right. These are probably the only 'easy' chairs in the house.

But the most traditional thing of all, and a sure sign that this is a 'respectable' home, is the Biblical text 'Be strong in the Lord' hanging beneath a copy of a famous Victorian oil painting.

NEWCASTLE TRAM

The coming of the trams was a sign of change in the outer suburbs of many cities. The houses in this photograph were built by wealthy Newcastle businessmen who did not want, or need, to live near their factories and offices. They had their own transport – originally carriages, by now cars.

But as city populations grew, housing developments began to reach out to once exclusive areas.

(Between 1900 and 1910, 60,000 people moved in to the suburbs around Birmingham.) Transport then became an essential service, as most of the new residents did not have their own.

Trams powered by overhead electric cables became a common sight. This Number 6 runs to the city centre via somewhere called 'Spital Tongues'! Perhaps the children waiting for the tram are on their way

to school, and the businessman, with his bowler hat and cane, is off to work. But does the big fat sack on the seat really belong to the lady sitting next to it? And, if so, what do you think is in it?

Not everything in this photograph points to modern developments. In the background, to the left of the tram, a herd of cattle is being driven to market – not something you are likely to see even on

A NEW HOME

Moving house is always an important event, and this couple and their son are posing rather self-consciously for a photograph in the living-room of their new home. All the flowers suggest that there is a garden – or perhaps they are gifts from the neighbours to make the newcomers feel welcome.

The wicker chairs are similar to those in the photographs on pages 18 and 24. And the chair nearest to the camera is a less elegant version of the dining chairs on page 19.

On the back of the husband's chair is a white antimacassar. This was to protect the upholstery from being stained by greasy hair oil. (Practi-cally all men used hair oil at this time.) Here the antimacassar seems to have been used only out of habit, because the back of the chair is not high enough for the man's head to touch it. And have you noticed that the chair in which his wife is sitting has no cushion at the back?

The family has a fine collection of ornaments – souvenirs, perhaps, of places they have visited on Bank Holiday outings. The cupboard on which many of them are displayed is 'built-in' between the chimney breast and the outside wall – so it would seem that the modern idea of built-in furniture is not so modern after all.

the outskirts of an industrial city today.

Have you spotted that there is something rather mysterious about this picture? The overhead power cables for the tram appear to continue out of the picture towards the photographer, but the tram lines themselves seem to stop at the crossroads. What happened to the tram, do you think, when it reached the corner?

STREETS OF BOLTON

(Above) The dreary, unimaginative development of Britain's industrial towns at the end of the nineteenth century is shown very clearly in this 1920s photograph of Bolton in Lancashire.

The long building in the centre of the picture and the big four-storey one on the left are factories, or 'works' as they were often called. Certainly the people living in these rows of identical houses do not have far to go to work, but neither can they get away from the smell of the works or the soot from their chimneys.

Attitudes to housing have changed. When these houses were first built at the end of the last century, they were a vast improvement on the slums that spoiled so many of Britain's industrial cities, and the people living in them were envied. Today, planners prefer a more flexible arrangement than these dull, monotonous streets.

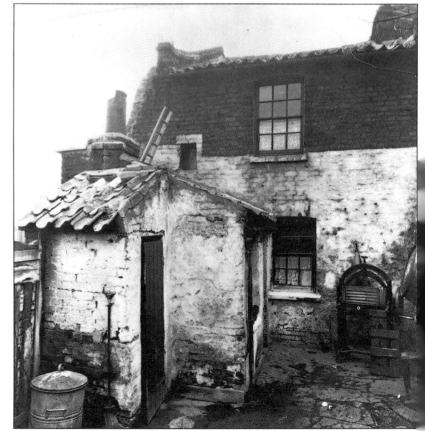

BREAKFAST OUTSIDE

What a contrast between this breakfast scene (right) and the two pictures opposite. This photograph, taken in 1928, shows how comfortable life could still be for those with money. Look at the silver egg cups and the silver-plated kettle on its tiny heater to keep the water hot. Although the woman is pouring the tea herself, there were probably servants to make it.

And look at the large fir tree, and the lawn sloping away into the distance. They suggest a large old house and grounds, perhaps lived in by the same family for many, many years.

SHOREDITCH

Although the house on the left looks like a cottage in the country, it is in fact in Shoreditch, in the East End of London. The photograph was taken in 1929, but somehow the scene seems little different from nearby Lamb Gardens, in Bethnal Green (page 12). Although there is 60 years between the two photographs, there is no noticeable improvement in the standard of housing.

The flaking paintwork on the walls and the dirty, broken paving stones, the outside lavatory near the dustbin and the tin bath hanging on the wall on the right all tell a story of continuing poverty and inadequate housing, despite several Acts of Parliament to try to improve slum areas.

The mangle against the back wall of the house is probably the only labour-saving device this family has – and there is no washing machine to help get the clothes clean before they are put through the mangle to remove the water.

A 'BARONIAL HALL'

The pictures on these two pages all show the same 'Baronial Hall', one of a number of different designs of house available on a private housing estate at Petts Wood, near Bromley in Kent.

Now Bromley is part of London's outer suburbs, but in the 1920s it was still in the country. The development of the area really took off after the opening of the railway station in 1928. The number of people using it increased so rapidly as a result of all the new housing that in 1932 the station had to be extended.

The houses were intended for professional people, who could afford to buy their own homes, and wanted to take their families away from the smoke and grime of the city. There were many developments like Petts Wood on the outskirts of towns and cities. The age of the commuter had arrived.

Outside view The Baronial Hall sold for what, today, seems the incredible price of £1,195 (eleven *hundred* and ninety five pounds!). And, as you can see, you got quite a large house for the money.

Look at the small panes of glass in the windows and the mock 'Tudor' timbering on the front gable. These timbers were purely decorative and no genuine Tudor beam would ever have been so straight and regular.

Notice, too, that although these are quite large houses and belonged to prosperous families, they have no garages – a sign that car ownership was still relatively rare.

The Hall The hall of the house echoes the architect's idea of 'Baronial Tudor'. This bears little resemblance to real Tudor architecture. Look at all the fake wooden panelling – it's on the walls, banisters and doors. And there are even timber ceiling 'beams'. Like those on the front of the house, they are decorative rather than useful.

The kitchen The kitchen is not quite as 'baronial'; by modern standards it is very basic. The sink is of stone, the floor looks rather slippery, there are no wipe-clean walls or units, and the cook has to walk across the kitchen carrying hot, heavy pans because there is no work-surface near the stove.

Standing under the window, neatly covered with a tablecloth, is a fold-away mangle for wringing out the washing – probably the only labour-saving device. Beside it is the coal scuttle; you can just see the front of the boiler between the cooker and the cupboard.

Somehow the room does not look much like a kitchen – perhaps because there are no pots and pans around, and no spice jars or knife racks hanging on the wall.

The sitting-room As befits a 'Baronial Hall', and the image the developers wanted to create, the sitting-room (or 'lounge' as it was often called) has a very spacious feel to it.

Fortunately the walls are not panelled like those in the hall (top), as this would make the room very dark. Instead the wallpaper, deep wooden picture rail and imposing fireplace are designed to match the panelling elsewhere.

The small table is set with the family's best silver-plate tea service. The lampshade is rather large, but at least it does not take as much light away as some of the others in this book – although no real Tudor home would ever have had anything like it!

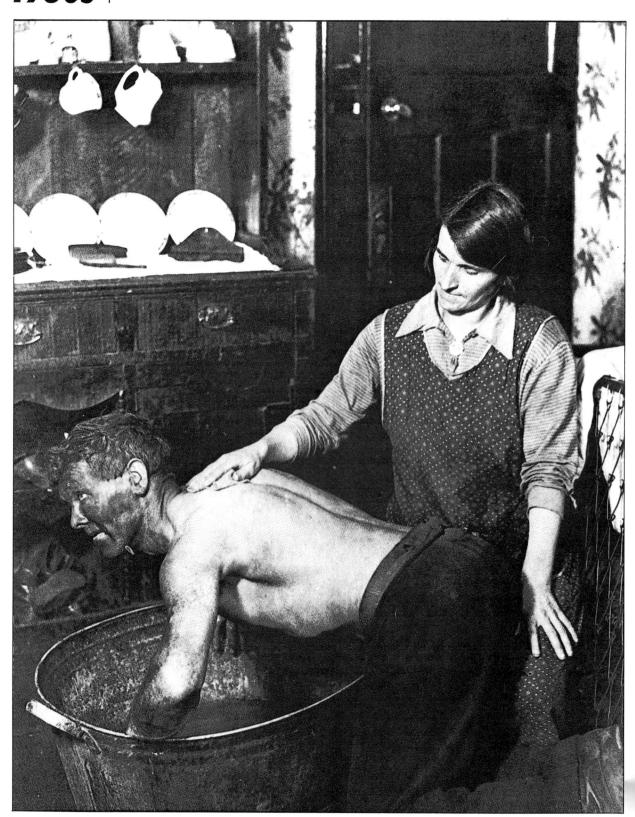

A MINER'S BATH

(Left) At the end of a hard day's work down the pit, a miner really needed a bath!

But it wasn't only miners for whom the bathroom was a tin bath in the living-room. This was all that most working-class homes had. There is one in the bottom photograph on page 30, and the rows of houses at the top of the same page would also have had baths like this. There may have been a scullery in which to put the bath, but in winter it was certainly much cosier to have it in front of the fire.

And, don't forget, the hot water for the bath did not come from a tap. It had to be heated on the fire, or in a special boiler which was part of the kitchen 'range' in many homes.

FARMWORKER'S COTTAGE

This couple (above) were photographed in their cosy living-room in Buckinghamshire in late 1939, just after the start of the Second World War (1939-45). So far the war has had little effect on them. As an agricultural worker the man will not have to join the armed forces. Growing as much food as possible was a vital part of the war effort.

Meanwhile the fire blazes cheerfully in the grate, polished with blacklead every day to keep it looking smart and glossily black. The surrounding bricks have been painted black – perhaps to stop them getting dirty. On one side of the hearth is a built-in cupboard, and on the other are shelves to display some of the family's 'best' china.

The sofa and armchair look really comfortable – about the first furniture in this book that does. Even the upholstered furniture of the wealthy Victorians looks too well stuffed and very hard to sit on. The pattern on the upholstery is interesting – with the recent revival of interest in the 1930s, quite a few modern designers have introduced fabrics with similar designs.

Along the mantelpiece are the family photographs. Do you think that the little girl in the photo third from the left embroidered the flowers on the mantel-cloth?

A TERRACE

The long terrace of houses on the left is in Widnes in Cheshire. Behind, you can see the roofs of a factory. The small, often badly built houses were probably put up by the factory owner in Victorian times to house his workers as cheaply as possible. It looks very like television's Coronation Street.

You can still find streets like this in Britain's industrial cities, although now the street lights will be electric rather than gas, and there will be cars parked beside the kerb and television aerials on the roofs.

A NEW ESTATE

This new estate of houses in Leicester (right) was probably built to replace a terrace much like the one on the left.

Although people have moved into the houses (notice the curtains in the windows), the state of the road and pavements suggests it is a very new development.

Local authorities up and down the country built housing estates like this in the 1930s, renting the houses out to people who could not afford to buy their own homes.

They are a great improvement on the earlier terraces. The houses have gardens at both front and back, the streets and pavements are wide, and there are trees in the background, not factories. Notice, too, that there is one central, compact chimney stack for each pair of houses – quite a contrast to the rows of chimneys on page 30.

COOKING THE MEAL

The houses in the street in Widnes opposite probably have kitchens very similar to this one (right), although when they were built cooking was done on a solid fuel 'range'. The gas cooker here is a recent introduction into what looks like a rather dark and cramped kitchen. And the size of the saucepans the woman is cooking with suggests that she has a large family to feed.

Look at the walls – apart from the tiles behind the cooker, they are just bare bricks painted over. In fact, the only hint of decoration in the room is in the way the edges of the old newspapers covering the shelves have been trimmed.

And the only cheerful thing is the woman's Union Jack apron. The photograph was taken in 1937, so perhaps the apron is a souvenir of the coronation of George VI that took place that year.

BOMB DAMAGE

It's easy to tell when this photograph was taken – in the 1940s, during the Second World War (1939-45).

In the right-hand corner is an air-raid shelter that seems to have survived the blast of the bomb that destroyed the two houses in the next road. All that remains standing is a little of the wall that divided them. The roof frame of the left-hand house is easy to identify, resting on the rubble of the house it once kept warm and dry.

The houses opposite are all badly damaged, with their windows broken, and their tiles and roofs collapsed. The house on the right does not look quite as bad, but that is because it did not have tiles on the wall between the top and bottom front windows.

Even though bomb damage like this has long since been repaired, you can often tell where bombs fell in cities. Walking along a street of identical houses, suddenly there is an open space or a few houses of a quite different, and generally more modern, style than the rest. Sometimes you can see the remains of the inside wall of a room, the mark of a fireplace or staircase. These are clues that a bomb landed where now there is an open area, or new houses stand.

A PREFAB

Finding houses for people whose homes had been destroyed by bombs was a big problem during the war. Money and building materials were in short supply, because all resources were concentrated on the war effort. Housing that was quick and cheap to put up was needed. The prefabricated houses shown here (right) – prefabs as they were always known – provided one answer. They were made of panels that could be quickly assembled on site.

Prefabs were not high-quality housing, and were intended only as a short-term solution to a pressing problem. They were expected to last only a few years – 10 was one official estimate – though you can still find them today in some areas, 40 years after the end of the war.

In the top picture you can see the shape of a roof and chimney on the wall at the end, showing where one row of houses used to join on to another. Probably the family in the prefab had once lived in an ordinary house in the same street.

Inside (bottom photo) the walls were very thin and, as you can see from the corner of the bedroom ceiling, the panels did not always fit very well. Prefabs were also quite small, often with only two bedrooms. Three little girls have to sleep in this bed with its old-fashioned iron frame.

Furniture was also a problem for families like this one – if they had been bombed out of their home, they had probably lost everything that was in it, too.

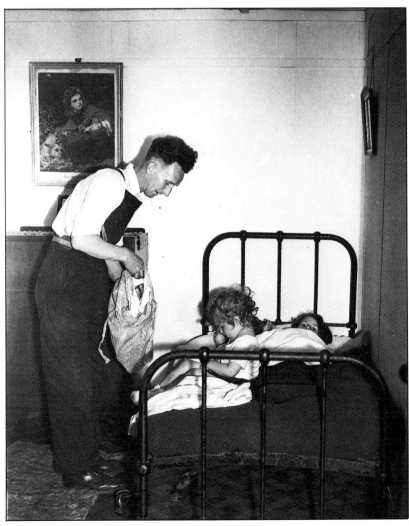

1950s

EAST END FLATS

The bombing of Britain's major cities during the Second World War destroyed many of the slum areas, but, as this photograph taken about 1950 shows, bad housing was still a problem after the war.

These flats in Wapping, in London's East End, were built in the 1890s to house the workers constructing Tower Bridge. (The tall building behind them is a huge Victorian warehouse.) They have the same barrack-like appearance as the Manchester tenements on page 16.

Look at the complicated system of pulleys and washing lines people have put up. This means that, even if they live in one of the upper storeys, and do not have a balcony, they can still get the washing out to dry. There's no frilly underwear on these clothes-lines, but have you spotted the pair of long underpants?

The rubble on the ground is probably the remains of another building that did not escape the bombs. You can see part of a wall behind the two women.

A NEW TOWN

(Right) Building new towns and rehousing people from crowded city areas was one way of dealing with the housing problem in cities. Although the development of new towns had first started at the end of the nineteenth century, it increased rapidly after the Second World War.

Names such as Hampstead Garden Suburb, Welwyn Garden City, Basildon New Town or, as here, Hemel Hempstead New Town, indicate what lay behind such developments: the idea of creating really pleasant places to live and work, that had been deliberately planned and built for this purpose. (Most towns and cities grow haphazardly according to the size of the population, which itself generally depends on the city's industries and so job opportunities.)

This development at Hemel Hempstead is much more attractive than the new estate in Leicester shown on page 37. The houses are not in one straight line. Instead they are 'stepped' to break the effect of a row and so give a less monotonous appearance. And there is a broad grass area between the pavement and the road.

Notice how bare the roofs look but it will not be long before television aerials start to appear on them.

A MINER'S HOUSE

This miner's home (left), photographed in Northumbria in 1953, contrasts well with the picture on page 34. It is typical of the homes of industrial workers at this time. The country's increasing prosperity meant better wages and more money to spend on things for the home.

On the table beside the bird's cage is the radio. Despite its large size, the quality of sound from it was probably not as good as that from today's tiny transistors. The lighting is, of course, electric, but the light-fitting with its ornamental glass shades has a hint of some of the oil and gas lamps in earlier photographs in this book. And the pattern on the wallpaper is so pale that it does not clash with the curtains – quite a contrast with interior decoration a century earlier.

Notice, too, the pelmet covered in the same material as the curtains. It, too, makes a change from the Victorian and Edwardian style of hanging curtains from large rings supported by a curtain rod – a style which is now coming back into fashion.

HOUSEWORK

Labour-saving devices like this vacuum cleaner did not catch on as quickly in Britain as they had done in the USA, where they were common from the 1920s onwards. In the 1920s and '30s, the middle and upper classes here had domestic servants to do the housework, though by the 1950s the 'daily' only came in twice a week. And for most of the working class such appliances were far too expensive, especially before the war when work was scarce and wages low.

After the war, the use of machines in the home began to increase, though only slowly at first. Today there are very few homes without labour-saving devices.

Look what a light, airy impression this room gives, although it is probably quite small. The pale, freshly painted walls ensure that the armchair, covered in dark 'leatherette' (imitation leather), and the ornate firescreen do not make the room gloomy.

In the bookcase you can just make out some paperbacks. These are some of the early Penguin books, with very plain covers. The first ones were published in the 1930s, and were the forerunners of all today's paperbacks.

BATHROOM GEYSER

A bathroom like this would have been beyond the wildest imaginings of even the most wealthy Victorians. In their day, maids carried jugs of hot water up to the bedrooms each morning and evening – you can see a washstand with its jug and basin in the corner of the bedroom on page 11.

This tiled bathroom has a 'Main New Junior' gas heater to supply the hot water, although the 'H' on one of the taps may indicate that, originally, hot water was piped to the bath from a boiler elsewhere.

BATHING THE BABY

Living conditions were not improving for everyone, as this photograph (right), taken in the mid-1950s, shows all too clearly. There is no bathroom in this woman's flat, and four families share this single basin. Soon the little girl will be too big to have her bath like this, and will have to go to the local public baths.

The walls look in a bad state. The paper on the right of the few tiles behind the basin has started to peel away where it gets splashed, and below the shelf there appears to be just bare plaster.

Lying on the shelf below the mirror you can just see a razor. Disposable razors had not yet been invented and electric ones were still unusual – and too expensive for the families living here, who not only had to share a basin, but a basin without any running hot water.

HIGH-RISE

These flats (above) at Hulme, Manchester, are the 1960s solution to the problem of overcrowding, just as the tenement blocks on page 16 had been in the 1890s.

Local housing authorities throughout the country saw building upward as the way to overcome housing problems like those on the previous page. In fact these 'tower blocks' are only 12 and 15 storeys high, while blocks of over 20 storeys were quite usual.

Some estates had a few 'low rise' blocks of the type you can see here, to act as a small-scale link between the tower blocks.

The idea of tower blocks was to combine as much housing with as much open space as possible. The flats at the top certainly had a splendid view. But tower blocks were seldom popular with the people who lived in them.

LOW-RISE

High-rise building was not the answer everyone hoped for. The brutal, anonymous blocks were easily vandalized. And if the lifts broke down – as they often did – how was a mother with small children, or an elderly person, going to get down from even the sixth storey, let alone the sixteenth?

More low-rise housing is the current trend. And, also important, is the increasing use of traditional building materials. The shell of these flats, at Leyton in east London, may be made in a factory using the most modern methods and materials; but you cannot see that beneath the facing of warm brick. Concrete slabs which faced many of the 1960s tower blocks, including those at Hulme (top), look raw and gaunt whatever the weather. They do not mellow and become homely in the way that brick and stone do.

1727 *Sensitivity of silver salts to light discovered*

1800 *Tom Wedgwood makes 'sun' pictures by placing leaves on specially treated leather and leaving them in the sun. The parts covered by the leaves did not darken like the rest and when they were removed their image remained on the leather*

1824 Portland cement invented by a Yorkshire bricklayer

1837 Queen Victoria comes to the throne

1848 Edwin Chadwick's Public Health Act provides for better drainage in towns and cities

1851 The Great Exhibition – gas cookers are one of the many novelties on display

1855 *Roger Fenton takes documentary photographs of the Crimean War*

1861 Mrs Beeton publishes her book of 'Household Management'

1875 Liberty's store in Regent Street, London, opens, specializing in the new, lighter style of furnishing that was increasingly fashionable Artisans' Dwelling Act allows local authorities to pull down and rebuild slum areas

1875-6 Large clearance and rebuilding scheme in Birmingham as a result of the Act. Corporation Street forms centrepiece of the redevelopment

1880s Port Sunlight on Merseyside is developed, with homes, churches, social clubs and schools

1883 'The Bitter Cry of Outcast London', a pamphlet condemning the appalling conditions for many of the capital's population

1884 Royal Commission on Housing is set up as a result of fuss caused by 'The Bitter Cry'

1888 *The first Kodak camera is produced Kodak processing service is set up by George Eastman*

1890s Reinforced concrete is first used in buildings

1892 *Cine film is perfected*

1898 Ebenezer Howard publishes 'Garden Cities for Tomorrow'

1901 Queen Victoria dies and Edward VII comes to the throne

1903 Work starts on building of Letchworth Garden City, influenced by Ebenezer Howard's work

1904 Rowntree Village Trust, on the outskirts of York, is founded

1905 First motor buses in service in London (Liverpool and Manchester had had electric trams for several years)

1907 Hampstead Garden suburb founded

1908 First 'Daily Mail' Ideal Home Exhibition Hand-worked automatic vacuum cleaners introduced

1910 Edward VII dies and George V becomes king

1914 First World War begins

1917 The first refrigerators go on sale in Britain

1918 First World War ends

1919 Housing and Town Planning Act makes local authorities responsible for the housing in their area

1929 *Flashbulbs for cameras are introduced, enabling pictures to be taken in poor light*

1930 Slum Clearance Act subsidizes landlords who rehouse tenants from slum areas

1935 *Kodachrome, the first modern film, goes on sale. In an improved version it is still used for slides*

1936 George V dies and George VI comes to the throne

1939 Second World War begins

1945 Second World War ends

1946 New Towns Act allows the creation of new urban centres for people from overcrowded city areas

1947 Town and Country Planning Act requires all new buildings to obtain planning permission *'Instant' polaroid cameras go on sale*

1952 George VI dies and Elizabeth II comes to the throne

1963 *Polaroid colour cameras go on sale Kodak introduce the first 'Instamatic' camera*

1969 *First photographs taken on the moon*

The entries in *italics* refer to developments in photography

Things to do

YOUR HOME'S HISTORY

Find out all you can about the house or block of flats in which you live. You'll probably be surprised at the number of changes that have taken place, even if your home is not very old. For example, installing central heating may have led to the blocking up of fireplaces and the removal of chimney pots. What about the windows – are they still the original ones? Have they been double-glazed? And what about the doors?

If the house is old, there could be people around who remember what it was like many years ago. Talk to them. What changes can they tell you about?

If you live in a brand new house or flat, it would be interesting to find out about the site on which it was built – was it agricultural land, waste-ground, or part of the garden of a large old house? Find out, too, about the planning procedures that were needed before your house could be built.

BUILDING MATERIALS

What type of building materials were used in your home, and in houses near you? If your home is old, what can you learn about traditional building materials and methods? Find out, too, if the style of building is a regional characteristic. What is the roof made of, the chimneys, the walls? What sort of doors does it have?

If your home is very new, why not find out about modern factory-built homes, the materials from which they are made, and how they are put up? See if you can discover how long your home took to build.

LOOKING AT ONE ROOM

Choose one room, the kitchen, sitting-room or bathroom perhaps, and find out how it has changed since the 1850s, when this book begins. Old paintings and photographs will give you many clues about things such as carpets, curtains and wall-papers, as well as furniture and light fittings.

You'll probably find that the way the room is used has also changed: the once formal 'front room' or drawing-room had gradually become today's relaxed sitting-room or lounge. (And if you think what the word 'lounge' means, it neatly sums up the change.)

You may be able to find old shop catalogues in your local reference library. These provide fascinating information about household goods in years gone by.

A PHOTOGRAPHIC ESSAY

Make a photographic record of your road or street as it is today (if you don't have a camera, make sketches).

Look out for all the interesting features: where one style of architecture changes to another, or where people have altered their houses to make them more individual. Compare the architecture with the photographs in this book. And don't forget what today's planners call street furniture – lamp-posts, litter baskets, seats and letter boxes. Make sure you caption the pictures clearly so you know exactly what they show.

VISITING OLD HOUSES

Many old houses are open to the public, and there is sure to be one not far from you that you can visit. The majority are large houses that belonged to the very rich – but you can still learn a lot from them about how people, both rich and poor, used to live.

Many of the houses have original furniture, decorations, ornaments and equipment from the period, and seeing these in place, it is easy to imagine what it must have been like living with them and using them. You can also often visit the kitchen and other work areas, and these can be especially fascinating.

The National Trust, founded in 1895, looks after many of these houses for the nation. If you write enclosing a stamped addressed envelope, they will send you details of National Trust houses in your area, and their times of opening. The address is:

The Junior Division
National Trust
P.O. Box 12
Westbury
Wiltshire BA13 4NA

Your local library will also be able help with information. And local papers, too, often include details houses that are open to the public.

e Victorian Home by Jenni Calder (B. T. Batsford)
:ollection of Victorian photographs covering all
)ects of home life during the period, although some
as, such as sanitary arrangements and servants'
arters, were of less interest than others to the
)sperous practitioners of the new art of
otography.

:torian Buildings of London 1837-87 by Gavin Stamp
d Colin Amery (Architectural Press)
specialized and rather technical book which is,
vertheless, fun to dip into, especially if you know
y of the buildings it discusses.

e Naughty Nineties by Angus Wilson (Eyre
ethuen)
:cellent pictures capture the atmosphere of the last
ars of Queen Victoria's reign, when the pace and
yle of society was set by the Prince of Wales (later
lward VII) and his friends.

fe in Victorian Britain by W. J. Reader
. T. Batsford)
fe in Edwardian Britain by Robert Cecil
. T. Batsford)
vo books which provide an overall picture of their
riod. They include information on changing social
:itudes and economic standards, both of which
'ected the life and homes of the people of the time.

ue World of the Forsytes by John Fisher (Secker and
arburg)
ised on the *Forsyte Saga* by John Galsworthy (and
e television series made from it). The author builds
a picture of the life led by the new rich in the early
rt of the century.

)und About a Pound a Week by Mrs Pember Reeves
.P Publishing)
eprint of a work first published in 1913, it is a survey
the poor district of Lambeth, south London. A
)neering work, it makes depressing reading. But it
·es provide an interesting insight into attitudes to
e poor at that time.

fe in Wartime Britain by E. R. Chamberlan
;. T. Batsford)
1other general survey of the period, in the same
·ries as *Life in Victorian Britain* (above).

Domestic Life in England by Norah Lofts (Weidenfeld
and Nicolson)
A well-illustrated survey of home life. There is a good
section on the period covered by this book.

English Stone Building by Alec Clifton Taylor and
A. S. Ireson (Victor Gollancz)
Although the book covers a much wider timescale
than just the last 130 years, there are a number of
interesting examples of buildings and architectural
styles from this period.

The English Home by Doreen Yarwood
(B. T. Batsford)
A history of the subject from Anglo-Saxon times until
1914, packed with interesting material.

The English Country Cottage by R. J. Browne (Hale)
The heyday of the English country cottage was
probably before Victorian times, but this is an
interesting book to dip into, not least because it
shatters the myth of the picturesque thatched cottage
with roses round the door found in so many
sentimental Victorian books and pictures.

Your local library and county records office are
probably also good sources of local information, and
may even have published a booklet about your area.
Many of them also have collections of old photographs
which you can see on application.

Index